WHAT THE F*@# SHOULD I DO WITH MY LIFE?

ANSWERS TO LIFE'S BIG QUESTION PLUS 50 JOBS TO GET YOU OFF YOUR MEDIOCRE A**

ZACH GOLDEN

RUNNING PRESS

PHILADELPHIA

Running Press

Hachette Book Group

1290 Avenue of the Americas, New York, NY 10104

www.runningpress.com

@Running_Press

Printed in China

First Edition: October 2019

Published by Running Press, an imprint of Perseus Books, LLC, a subsidiary of Hachette Book Group, Inc. The Running Press name and logo is a trademark of the Hachette Book Group.

The Hachette Speakers Bureau provides a wide range of authors for speaking events. To find out more, go to www.hachettespeakersbureau.com or call (866) 376-6591.

The publisher is not responsible for websites (or their content) that are not owned by the publisher.

Print book cover and interior design by Joshua McDonnell

Library of Congress Cataloging-in-Publication Data has been applied for.

ISBNs: 978-0-7624-9634-1 (hardcover), 978-0-7624-9635-8 (ebook)

TLF

10 9 8 7 6 5 4 3 2 1

INTRODUCTION

I'm something of a job aficionado. To date, I've worked as a dishwasher, prep cook, author, film director, retail associate, checkout lady, knife salesman, underage illegal alcohol sales bait, camp counselor, retail buyer, snowboard coach, advertising writer, lawn mower, sporting goods store manager, barista, babysitter, trampoline safety attendant, and television producer; plus I had an internship at an ad agency that only marketed pharmaceutical products, because regular advertising wasn't morally callous enough. And in my employed lifetime, I've become a self-proclaimed expert in just about everything having to do with jobs, from labor relations and work-life balance to fabricating intricate yet believable excuses for missing work for extended periods of time. Finding a new career is one of the most difficult decisions we face in our lives. Fortunately, with my breadth of experience, generosity, and strong sense of entitlement, there is this at-times helpful guide that takes the important decision out of your weak, impotent hands and helps you figure out what the fuck you should do with your life.

What the fuck should you do with your life? Answer the ten questions below honestly and with the fear of the Christian God in your heart, and you'll get an answer.

1. How important is your earnings potential to your choice in career?
   (A) I just want to help people and feel satisfied
   (B) I want to not worry about money and be able to afford yearly sex-tourism trips to the South Pacific
   (C) I'm a 4, so I need to be extremely rich to attract a mate
   (D) I am only looking for fuck-you money and will do anything to amass it

2. What is your favorite Star Wars film?
   (A) *A New Hope*
   (B) *The Empire Strikes Back*
   (C) *Return of the Jedi*
   (D) Wrong

3. Which of the following statements best reflects your ability to work while high on drugs?
   (A) Nobody would be able to tell the difference
   (B) I'd be nervous but confident that I could pull it off
   (C) I'd be freaking out, man
   (D) I'd attack and injure my boss with nail clippers

4. How important is it to you to help people with your work?
   (A) Extremely important—I'm not a total pile of shit
   (B) Important as long as all my wants and needs are accounted for first
   (C) Not a consideration
   (D) People are a commodity meant to be exploited by the cunning and morally superior capitalist

5. On a scale of 1 to 10, how attractive do you think you are? (Subtract 2 from your answer to accommodate reality.)
   (A) 1–3
   (B) 4–6
   (C) 7–9
   (D) 10

6. True or false: the New England Patriots are a bunch of no-good, dirty cheaters, and anybody who roots for them is a trash-garbage human being.
   (A) True
   (B) True

7. Would you be comfortable doing something professionally that violated your morals?
   (A) Definitely not
   (B) Probably not
   (C) How much money we talkin'?
   (D) I already work in finance

8. How rich are your parents?
   (A) Poor
   (B) Middle class
   (C) Rich
   (D) "Donated" $2.5 million just to get my middling ass into Harvard

9. My coworkers or peers would describe me as:
   (A) Selfless
   (B) Highly capable
   (C) Impotent
   (D) The person who got arrested for setting up hidden cameras in the bathroom

10. Which of the following cities can suck a dick?
    (A) Boston

Add up your score by giving yourself 1 point for every question you answered A, 2 points for every B, 3 points for every C, and 4 points for every D; then forget all of it because there's no such thing as the perfect job for you. Every job is garbage and will make you miserable, and we're all just specks of dust hurtling through space trying to delay our inevitable deaths. Good luck!

Lose any remaining faith in humanity by working as a fucking Retail Associate

Retail associates will soon be replaced by robots that are more efficient than humans, at least until the rebellion, but until then, they're an important position that's equal parts sales, customer service, and getting belittled by uppity whites. A career as a retail associate isn't particularly lucrative, but what you sacrifice in wages, you'll more than make up for in the feelings of murderous rage when you compromise all your morals daily, because the customer is always right. You'll sell almost nothing, because the only customers you'll deal with are only at the store to see the product in person before they buy it online for cheaper and without human contact. The only customers who won't scurry away from you like roaches when the lights are turned on are the elderly, who are confused by the internet and thus genuinely need your help, and small, angry people who hate themselves but are too self-absorbed to admit it, so they go to a store and take it out on you instead.

HOW TO BECOME A RETAIL ASSOCIATE

Go into a store you'd be interested in working at and loudly announce anything that you'd do differently if you were in charge; then ask for a job application but say it sort of sarcastically and sigh like it's beneath you. If you find this doesn't work, try bolstering your résumé or CV with "relevant experience" by listing a friend's number as your former employer; then have them shower you in accolades and superlatives, and watch the job offers come rolling in.

QUALIFICATIONS

- You have no problem striking up a conversation with a stranger, even though every stranger is a potential murderer

- You aspire to be an entrepreneur but lack the drive

- A love of petty drama

OCCUPATIONAL HAZARDS

- Poverty

- A never-ending loop of Top 40 music that will slowly lull you into sociopathy

- If you don't viciously kiss their asses, customers will ask to speak to your manager, who will have to mercifully fire you to assuage them

Don't want to routinely debase yourself for minimum wage? Go to page 53.

Glide majestically above all lesser vehicles by becoming a fucking Hovercraft Pilot

Earth is a combination of land, water, and air, and hovercrafts are the only vehicles on the planet able to dominate all these surfaces at will, making them the number one escape vehicles for whatever mass extinction event will eventually befall humanity. Hovercrafts glide effortlessly nine inches above whatever surface they feel like conquering, propelled by giant fans and the calm, steady hand of one of the world's most underappreciated professionals, the hovercraft pilot. There are professional drivers, boat captains, and aircraft pilots, all of whom are respected despite specializing in only one vehicle, like goddamn cowards. Hovercraft pilots are experts in—or at least have lots of false confidence about—driving, boating, and flying, and they also should be proficient in wrestling gators, just in case. Hovercrafts can go places no other vehicle can, provided there are no obstructions taller than nine inches, and hovercraft pilots are heroic lifelines in some of life's most serious situations, such as search-and-rescue emergencies, military operations, and making Florida seem like a bearable place to spend any amount of time.

HOW TO BECOME A HOVERCRAFT PILOT

More than any other job in this book, the life of a hovercraft pilot is more a calling than a career. If you are destined to become one, you will know, and nobody will have to tell you what to do, because it will possess your soul and control your mind and body, and you will either become a hovercraft pilot or die trying, for it is your reason for existing.

QUALIFICATIONS

....

- Preordained destiny as a chosen one
- Oakley Blade sunglasses

OCCUPATIONAL HAZARDS

....

- Hovercrafts are the ultimate pheromone: you will become irresistible to anyone with even a modicum of good taste

- Occasionally pilots are sucked into the giant fans and sliced into hundreds if not thousands of tiny pieces, which is almost always fatal

You're a fucking coward? Go to page 73.

Witness the steady decline of our educational system firsthand by becoming a fucking Teacher

Teachers are tasked with one of the most important jobs in the world: preparing the youth for what lies ahead, a Mad Max–ian dystopian future in which he/she/they who control the water control everything. Teachers take you in at five years old, when you know almost nothing of worth, and in thirteen years, they fill your brain with enough knowledge to be a contributing member of society. With all this responsibility, education, training, and influence over countless children's lives, if you become a teacher, you will get paid just enough to only need to bus tables at Applebee's four nights a week to afford the lease payments on your Kia Rio. All that you need to know about becoming a teacher is this: tenure. Once you get it, you're pretty much untouchable. If they want to get rid of you, they have to jump through so many bureaucratic hoops and fill out so much soul-crushing paperwork that as long as you don't punch somebody out or love kids in the wrong way, all you have to do is show up, and you're set until retirement.

HOW TO BECOME A TEACHER

Go approximately $200,000 in debt getting bachelor's and master's degrees, student-teach for a semester while living in your car, get a full-time job offer that's an hour and forty minutes away from your home, and hang on for dear life until you get tenure and can fuck shit up.

QUALIFICATIONS

- You aren't in it for the money, because there is none

- You want summers off

- The restraint to not hit children, even if they really deserve it

OCCUPATIONAL HAZARDS

- Betsy DeVos

- You will pay into a pension that you will one day lose to somehow benefit a wealthy white man

Hate all children? Go to page 51.

Tell people to strip down to their underwear at work with no repercussions by becoming a fucking Medical Doctor

Doctors go to school for fifteen years so that for the rest of their lives, anytime a person refers to them as Mr. or Mrs., they can insist on their proper title and feel a smug sense of moral superiority. There are many different types of MDs, but all share one incredible power: they can write prescriptions for drugs. Marijuana, opioids, benzos, you name it—if you give up the prime years of your life and dedicate them to medicine and science, these drugs can all be yours with just a signature. But being a doctor isn't just drug-fueled sex parties; occasionally it can also be a lot of work with very long hours. Every day, you'll have to deal with patients who babble on and on about their problems and never want to hear about how you're doing, as well as nurses and admins who are beneath you since they didn't work a little harder and become doctors. You'll get paid a lavish amount of money but won't have any time to spend it because all you'll do is work, and your marriage will fail because your spouse feels like you're married to your job, but hey, at least you drive an Audi and are better than everyone else.

HOW TO BECOME A MEDICAL DOCTOR

After getting a bachelor's degree, you'll go to a four-year medical school, during which time you should act like you're already a doctor among all family and friends so that they get used to the idea of you being in a higher caste than they are. Finally, you complete a three- to seven-year residency, and by the time you're thirty-six and just past your fuckable years, you're a doctor, and it's all drugs, money, and yachts.

QUALIFICATIONS

- You aspire to be a drug dealer but can't help how good you look in a lab coat

- You want to be rich but still carry a pager

OCCUPATIONAL HAZARDS

- Malpractice, even if you insist it was an accident

- You will have no free time, and all interpersonal relationships will inevitably crumble under the weight of your career

- Starting and supporting a nationwide opioid epidemic

You're fucking stupid? Go to page 61.

Be continually disgusted by the human body by becoming a fucking Masseuse

Adult bacne, excess body hair, fat folds, stretch marks, cellulite, skin tags, and hairy moles are just a few of the characters in the hellscape that is the average human body. As a masseuse, you not only have to touch all these things and more, you must rub your client's mangled nude carcass for an hour (or ninety minutes if they're rich), all while not becoming visibly or audibly ill, as it ruins the mood. The only good reason to ever give a massage is to get a massage immediately after. For a masseuse, this will never be the case. Life will be a massage train where you're always the caboose; your rub will forever go unrubbed. All is not lost, however, as most of your clients will choose to go nude; this presents two opportunities for the enterprising young masseuse: you can take secret photos of their grotesque bodies and use them as collateral for blackmail, or you can prey upon man's greatest massage-related fear—being accused of acting sexually untoward during a session, which is usually good for some hush money at the very least.

HOW TO BECOME A MASSEUSE

During a transitional period in your life, give a casual, reassuring backrub to a good friend that you haven't seen in a while who looks like they could use it. While they are pouring their heart out to you, they'll reveal that they're going through a really dark time and haven't gotten out much lately. You'll get bored and distract yourself by thinking about your problems and how you should be getting paid for this since it's so boring and you're doing all the work, so you make a mental note and get licensed, and that's that.

QUALIFICATIONS

- You're not easily disgusted by the human body
- You don't need to take a break after three minutes of rubbing because your hands are tired
- You do not have sharpened scissors or knives for hands

OCCUPATIONAL HAZARDS

- Men
- Sudden blindness from bodies with Medusa-like effects
- Insanity spurred on by a perpetual loop of relaxing Japanese music

Have weak, childlike hands that lack the grip strength necessary for massage therapy? Go to page 35.

Be routinely told to fuck off and die by strangers by becoming a fucking Telemarketer

Telemarketing combines two things that everyone loves: talking on the phone to strangers at inconvenient times and being pushily sold shit that you don't want or need. Thus, as a telemarketer, you're expected to be successful approximately 2 percent of the time. This means that 98 percent of your job is getting hung up on and being called deeply personal, hurtful names by people who are rightfully annoyed that you bothered them even though they definitely are on the Do Not Call list, while the other 2 percent is spent robbing the elderly of their last dollars and speaking to the saddest, loneliest people on the planet, who will seize on any phone call as an opportunity for human contact, which to them is rare and fleeting, leaving you shook. The companies using telemarking know it doesn't work, but it's cheap enough that they don't care, because what if it did? This is made possible by paying minimum wage, plus commission, which is nothing because you will never sell anything, and renting offices lit exclusively by flickering fluorescent lights and that somehow always smell like someone recently microwaved shrimp.

HOW TO BECOME A TELEMARKETER

The beauty of telemarketing—and you really have to squint to see it—is that they will hire anyone, from infants who have yet to develop speech or object permanence to confused elderly people who accidentally wandered in to the office thinking it was a RadioShack and never left. If you can show up on time-ish, read a script, and get hung up on, you're overqualified and should probably find another line of work. But when you get fired from *that* job and have no other options, take solace in knowing you can always fall back on telemarketing.

QUALIFICATIONS

OCCUPATIONAL HAZARDS

- It's extremely common for telemarketers to develop an unconscious psychosexual desire for rejection

- Poverty

- Impotence

Had your tongue cut out as punishment for snitching? Go to page 5.

Make stuff people hate by becoming a fucking Advertising Creative

Advertising creatives come up with the ideas for ads and then spend the next six months watering those ideas down through an endless death march of client calls, legal reviews, and revisions, until their once-precious ideas turn into the nonsensical garbage you see on TV and also everywhere else. It's a job that gives you the illusion of being an artist with the paycheck and day-to-day of a finance bro. You'll work long days, late nights, weekends, and holidays, devoting all your creative energy to hoodwinking the masses into buying shit for the benefit of a gigantic, awful corporation that stands in opposition to everything you believe in. There's nothing sadder than an old person in advertising, bitter and beaten down from years of having to pretend to know what's relevant among the youth. It's a young person's game, which is why you'll be paid handsomely until you are forty-five and then put out to pasture making those deeply unsettling Charmin ads with the family of cartoon bears with the dingleberry problem, until you can't take it anymore.

HOW TO BECOME AN ADVERTISING CREATIVE

Put together a portfolio of your work; send the portfolio to ad agencies you'd like to work for; score a meeting with their creative director, a fourteen-year-old Swedish boy who's an influencer on Kik; vibe with him over *Fortnite* or *Frozen* or whatever kids are into these days; and spin that into a job offer that will rob you of all your artistic ambition.

QUALIFICATIONS

- Being able to bullshit extemporaneously like a psychopath luring their next victim

- You've always fancied yourself as "artsy" but lack any real drive or ambition

- Self-control not to explode at clients, who are the dumbest people in the world—trust me, we did a study

OCCUPATIONAL HAZARDS

- You'll start out a bright-eyed, aspiring artist and be spit out the other end an upper-middle-class suburban Republican who dresses twenty years too young and carries a vape pen

- All your coworkers will be young, successful-ish, and unhappy, so adultery is prodigious

Have artistic integrity? Go to page 65.

Wear white after Labor Day and get away with it by becoming a fucking Chef

We have to eat in order to not die, and chefs are at the forefront of making the process of not dying from starvation far more enjoyable. Chefs lead the kitchen, working with their hands, solving problems, and developing dishes that delight diners or at the very least don't result in the county board of health shutting down the restaurant due to an apparently wanton desire to poison the masses. It's a wonderful career, except for the fact that you're serving people, as opposed to, say, dogs, and people pull shit like "gluten allergy, soy okay" or send back a perfectly cooked piece of meat just because they're a tire fire of a human being that needs to wield power and control over strangers that they're lacking in their own life, and you can't do anything about it, because if a customer catches even a whiff of discontent from the chef, they will leave an eviscerating one-star review on some garbage social media platform that's really a pyramid scheme started by two finance bros who are into microdosing, and your business will be ruined forever.

HOW TO BECOME A CHEF

Practice your chef's kiss until it's the chef's kiss of chef kisses. Ask to speak to the executive chef of a restaurant you'd be interested in working at, and when you meet them, show off your skillful kiss. He (or she, but probably he) will be impressed with your mastery of the profession's most important skill and offer you a job on the spot, and you will rise through the ranks, dedicating yourself to cooking while working until midnight six days a week while somehow still being flat-ass broke, and then one day your executive chef will die from mixing benzodiazepines with alcohol and ketamine, and you'll be next in line for the promotion, but you won't get it because the restaurant's owner wanted to "mix it up" by hiring his nephew instead.

QUALIFICATIONS

- An ability not to pass out in humid 120°F kitchens while doing physical labor with no breaks for ten hours a day, six days a week
- White is your color

OCCUPATIONAL HAZARDS

- Likelihood of fatal grease fire higher than most other professions
- You're at the mercy of worthless food critics, though the chef's code specifies you should try to poison them at every opportunity

Need to be in charge but fucking suck at cooking? Go to page 31.

Make the world a better place by becoming a fucking

Lawyer

Lawyering isn't what *Law & Order* would have you believe. Most lawyers rarely, if ever, go to trial, and those who do are just living a hollow existence in the shadow of District Attorney Jack McCoy, played expertly by the incomparable, versatile, and distinguishably handsome Sam Waterson, America's finest legal mind. You will be extremely overworked and will either get paid lavishly to help awful rich people and corporations skirt the law without consequence or get paid dogshit to actually do good and pursue justice—your choice. Law is one of the three professions approved by Jewish mothers, alongside medicine and, of course, old-timey money lending.

And there are many great opportunities that lawyering will afford you; for example, if you defend a definitely not-guilty former football star (go Bills!) exonerated of murdering his ex-wife and a waiter, you can spin that into obscene fame for the whole family. You'll also make valuable contacts in the world of crime, leaving you many options should you ever decide to pursue a different career, which you will, because being a lawyer will suck the life out of you.

HOW TO BECOME A LAWYER

Be a petulant, argumentative child. Adults will tell you, "You should be a lawyer," which you'll take literally, but which is really a nicer, more encouraging way of saying, "I hate you and want you to be miserable for many, many years." Go to college, then lawyer college, pass a bunch of boring exams, and then compete with the other 1.34 *million!* lawyers in these United States for the handful of good jobs available, which you won't get, so you'll be a soulless ambulance chaser instead.

QUALIFICATIONS

- You can't lose an argument and are the type of person who will edit Wikipedia articles to prove you're right
- You should probably own a suit

OCCUPATIONAL HAZARDS

- Phone calls at 4:00 a.m. from friends you haven't heard from in a long time to bail them out of jail for a "misunderstanding" with a prostitute
- Having your feelings hurt— everyone hates lawyers, but they're people, too, guys

Have something to contribute to the world? Go to page 75.

Hopefully don't get electrocuted to death while working as a fucking Electrician

As an electrician, you can make a good, honest living just about any place that has electricity, and you can make an absolute killing in places without electricity by convincing the masses that you created it and that they must worship you as their lightning king. You work with your hands, solve problems, and fix dangerous messes caused by laughably overconfident people with DIY Pinterest boards and lifetimes of white privilege that make them mistakenly believe they are capable of anything. Electricians routinely work with live wires containing enough voltage to kill them instantly. The most common last words for an electrician are, "I wonder if this wire is hot," and then shitting themselves. But electricians have lots of job security, unless the plot of the failed NBC drama *Revolution* is prophecy and there's a permanent worldwide electrical blackout caused by a start-up that was trying to "disrupt electricity" but ended up doing literally that—then they're fucked. Electricians, like all proud tradespeople, are duty-bound to criticize any and all work done by previous electricians, irrespective of merit. They will do the same to you—there's a mutual understanding; it will all be in the welcome packet.

HOW TO BECOME AN ELECTRICIAN

In order to not kill yourself and others, electricians must apprentice for five years, at which point your mentor will take you on a spa weekend and buy you a nice dinner, but the power will go out and everyone will gasp and someone will yell, "Is anybody here an electrician?" And your mentor will take you by the hand and look into your eyes and say, "He is."

QUALIFICATIONS

- Must look good in boot-cut light-wash jeans from the early nineties
- GED or a high school diploma, if you want to be a show-off

OCCUPATIONAL HAZARDS

- Electricity
- North Korean hackers hell-bent on disabling the power grid
- Basically everything you'll be doing, every second of the day

Afraid of work-related death? Go to page 9.

Drink Mylanta straight from the bottle after becoming a fucking Air Traffic Controller

Air traffic controllers are the ones responsible for planes not routinely crashing into each other and becoming blazing infernos falling out of the sky as they claim lives and cause super-annoying travel delays for the living. It's one of the most stressful jobs in the world, because in addition to having to work at an airport, a bad day on the job means 170,000+ pounds of steel, tiny liquor bottles, and assorted human parts got scattered somewhere they shouldn't have, and man, oh man, that's gonna be a lot of paperwork. To protect the safety of the thousands of lives resting on their shoulders, air traffic controllers are drug-tested more than a professional football player who angered thirty-one "old-fashioned" billionaires (and also Mark Davis) by daring to protest the unlawful murder of African Americans by the police. All air traffic controllers are forced to retire at fifty-six, but you'll be so burned out by then that you won't care. You will adjust to the newfound lack of control in your life by ordering around your family, who will begin to resent you and wish you were back in the tower, and you'll wish that too, but it will be impossible because you're far too old and demented.

HOW TO BECOME AN AIR TRAFFIC CONTROLLER

Becoming an air traffic controller takes many months or years—or half of a three-day weekend, if you're really smart like me. You'll practice on simulators until you're able to consistently not kill everyone; then you'll be drug-tested, psychologically tested, physically tested, and asked really seriously, "Are you sure you want to do this to yourself and your family? The pay is not that great." And if you pass all the tests, a lifetime of stress ulcers and living next to the airport awaits you.

QUALIFICATIONS

- Must be younger than thirty-one years old when first hired and preferably at least a 5 or drunk 7

- A strong mustache is essential for the job, even for women, so that everyone knows who's in charge here

OCCUPATIONAL HAZARDS

- Your friends and family will never see you because you're busy preventing catastrophe

- Airport and airport-adjacent dining options are usually quite limited and unhealthy, making it difficult to take a two-hour lunch where you can recharge and get some much needed you time

Think 9/11 was an inside job? Go to page 95.

Please don't become a fucking Politician

You get into politics for one of two reasons: there's a cause you are passionate about and politics is the most direct avenue to effect change, or you're a power-hungry narcissist who should be chemically castrated so that your bloodline mercifully ends with you for the benefit of all humanity. Regardless of your intentions, a career in politics will turn you into a shit-eating shell of a human who only exists to spew poll-tested talking points and disagree with whatever the other side is doing, while bending over for billionaires and corporations owned by billionaires so that they'll bankroll your pointless existence until the public inevitably turns against you when they discover that you're a fraud, a sexual predator, or, worse, a New England Patriots fan. Politicians in the United States have the dumbest employer in the known universe, the American public. But to attain power, you'll have to meet them and give them a bunch of boring speeches about things that you'll never accomplish, and they'll touch you and tell you their boring problems, and you have to feign empathy and pretend to care about their insignificant little lives so that they vote for you, but once you're voted in, fuck those assholes—you can do whatever you want until you're up for reelection.

HOW TO BECOME A POLITICIAN

Have a rich, powerful white father who's either in politics or the CEO of a major corporation who pays your way to an Ivy League education and then leans on his contacts to get you a cushy job where you earn seven figures and bide your time. Daddy will manufacture sexually compromising evidence against the governor, whom he will then blackmail into resigning, but not before naming you replacement governor by executive order. If you don't have or can't acquire that type of daddy, I don't fucking know; run for school board or something.

QUALIFICATIONS

- Doctor's note showing a clinical diagnosis of narcissistic personality disorder or sociopathy
- You feel, like, really strongly about stuff, guys

OCCUPATIONAL HAZARDS

- Assassination attempts and/or successes
- Power will infect you like a cancer and consume you until you can't take it anymore and quit to take a job as a lobbyist

You're not a total piece of shit? Go to page 43.

Eventually be replaced by drones after becoming a fucking Postal Worker

The postal system is amazing. People take for granted that you can stuff just about anything into an envelope, and for fifty cents the postal service will deliver it anywhere in the country—even the really shitty parts that nobody cares about—in about three days, and it will get there basically every single time, except for when you really, really need it and obsessively track it online; then it will be inexplicably lost or delayed, guaranteed. Postal workers are the backbone of the system, at least until they're replaced by artificially intelligent robots or Trump Mail®, which only hires nonunion 8s and above who will sign nondisclosure agreements. Postal workers sort and deliver our mail, sass customers at post offices, and, of course, work tirelessly to cover up the existence of email, mail's single greatest threat. It's an incredibly important job that pays well but not nearly enough for all the shit you'll have to put up with. Postal workers serve the same community, often for decades at a time; they watch children grow up and new families come and go, and they provide a vital service, but nobody will bother to learn your name, treat you like a human being, or intervene when a pack of dogs finally, after years of planning, attacks and tears you limb from limb.

HOW TO BECOME A POSTAL WORKER

Postal work is a highly unionized field, so aspirants must break in the traditional way: stalking and kidnapping an existing employee, forging doctors' notes, forcing them to call in sick for two weeks, and then assuming their identity and telling any suspicious coworkers that you used the last two weeks to get some much-needed cosmetic surgery, which somehow also resulted in amnesia, so you might have some questions.

QUALIFICATIONS

- Must look good in shorts
- Must watch every episode of The Inspectors and be able to speak about its greater themes and story arcs at length extemporaneously

OCCUPATIONAL HAZARDS

- Al Gore and his stupid internet
- You are frequently the person who discovers the body on Law & Order

Love dogs and don't want to become their sworn blood enemy?
Go to page 41.

Eventually fail at trying to become a fucking Filmmaker

Filmmaking is one of the few careers where you can make two things a decade and still be considered productive. That's because unless you're one of the exceedingly few who've already hit it big or are the child of a famous actor, producer, or director, you have almost no chance of earning a living making movies. You'll spend years begging every family member, friend, and professional acquaintance you know for money to fund your film, but none of them will give you a dime because backing a film is about as smart an investment as setting your money on fire and oftentimes not nearly as entertaining. Getting a film made is a lot like starting a Ponzi scheme: you make a lot of promises that you have no ability to keep and hope that somehow it all works out in the end or that people will forget they gave you their time or money. If you do manage to get your film made, it will be a thrill but also knock three years off of your life expectancy. But don't worry; you'll probably fail long before that's a problem.

HOW TO BECOME A FILMMAKER

Go to the bar of a Ritz-Carlton; there will be a weeping elderly woman four drinks into the afternoon. Sit across from her and order a Tom Collins, which was her late husband's drink (if they don't make a Tom Collins, make a scene until they do; it's what he would have done). She will strike up a conversation. Play it cool, and casually mention that you're a filmmaker, and she'll tell you that she and her husband met at some depressing old cinema, and it will start to get emotional. Find out everything about her late husband, Morty, and become him; that's now your thing. She will eventually view you as a newer, better Morty, and through a lot of cajoling and psychosexual manipulation, you'll get her to fund your movie despite her gut feeling that it's not a wise investment.

QUALIFICATIONS

- Can do the proper French pronunciation of Godard and proves it by bringing him up constantly
- You are pathologically controlling to the detriment of every other part of your life outside work

OCCUPATIONAL HAZARDS

- Inevitable failure
- Poverty
- The whole world *is* against you

Not independently wealthy? Go to page 19.

Design buildings people will hate by becoming a fucking Architect

Architects design buildings by drawing detailed plans that dictate aesthetic choices and the structure necessary in order to not spontaneously collapse upon itself during a particularly rowdy quinceañera, ironically killing fifteen partygoers. They then spend years having their vision destroyed by ignorant clients who conflate having money with having taste, impotent bureaucrats they subconsciously fantasize about murdering, and contractors who cut every possible corner yet somehow still finish five months late, resulting in a final building that's an empty generic husk of the original design and that will be compared unfavorably to the work of Frank Geary, who, besides Art Vandelay, is the only architect anyone has ever heard of. In order to attract high-end clients, architects need to appear cultured and worldly, typically through a vast collection of expensive coffee-table books and questionable choice in nonprescription glasses. They also must be extremely skilled at technical drawing, so good that they're effortlessly able to draw unflattering photorealistic nudes of their enemies that can be used to drum up business or to silence witnesses in the event of a building collapse.

HOW TO BECOME AN ARCHITECT

Begin frequenting the highest-end nightclubs in your area and looking for the crassest rich asshole you can find; this will undoubtedly be a real estate developer. Befriend the developer by offering cocaine, but switch it with meth, and lead them on a drug-fueled night of debauchery that you'll chronicle and catalog with your extemporaneous technical drawings and probably some photos and video, just to be safe. From there, it's just some good old-fashioned quid pro quo extortion, and then you've got yourself a building to design.

QUALIFICATIONS

- Unflattering glasses
- Must have a fun foreign name that rolls awkwardly off the tongue
- Can pull off a scarf even in the summer

OCCUPATIONAL HAZARDS

- The "three strikes and you're out" rule for building collapses
- If you are really successful, you'll be called a "starchitect," and that's just awful
- Your clients will be primarily unbearable rich people

Look like a giant penis when you wear a hard hat? Go to page 37.

Make hair did by becoming a fucking Hairdresser

Any profession in which you're expected to casually converse with relative strangers and pretend to care about what they're saying should be approached with extreme skepticism. When you're a hairdresser, your clients will open up to you and trust you with their appearance and, over years of loyal patronage, their deepest and darkest secrets. Then, without any warning and for no apparent reason, they'll leave you like a dad who's just going out for cigarettes, and you'll never hear from them again, but years later you'll spot them at a supermarket at 11:30 p.m., and even though you'll be the only two customers there, you'll both pretend not to see each other. There is almost no margin for error in hairdressing. If you give a client one bad haircut, they'll be extremely not understanding, even if you've given them dozens of not-terrible haircuts prior to the offending one, like you're not allowed to have an off day once in a while. You'll work exclusively with insane people who act like they're on a reality show and are able to conjure petty drama like a mutant power, and you'll never have any job security. And even though there is a ten-to-one ratio of women to men, the most famous, successful, high-earning hairdressers, the ones with the shampoos and corporate endorsement deals, are overwhelmingly . . . men! Congratulations, guys—we did it again.

HOW TO BECOME A HAIRDRESSER

Be an angsty teenager who smoked cigarettes out in front of the high school just so passersby could see how different you are and how much you don't care about society's norms and conventions. Dye your hair an unnatural color, get a piercing you'll later regret, and go to cosmetology school. Then sweep hair for a year until Eduardo, a talented but unreliable stylist who has yet to realize his full potential, doesn't show up for his shift, and when his client arrives, you step in and confidently say, "I'll do it," and then you mangle that person's hair, but don't worry—eventually you'll get the hang of it.

QUALIFICATIONS

- You're not driven mad by the sound of other people's voices
- Ability to lie convincingly right to a person's face

OCCUPATIONAL HAZARDS

- You'll be the first person to tell men they're balding, and they may become violent
- Lice

Have resting bitch face? Go to page 13.

Develop severe orthopedic problems by becoming a fucking Computer Person

When you're a computer person—be it a software engineer, developer, programmer, IT support staff, or grand wizard—normals don't understand what you do, beyond the fact that you're good with computers and might have Asperger's. Computering careers are a house of cards built on a foundation of this mass ignorance. You will get paid handsomely to do something involving computers, presumably so that normals don't have to do it, because they're unable. Computer people will almost certainly be the ones to save the planet from North Korean super-hackers hell-bent on total destruction, thus becoming a revered class of demigods who rule the world, until advanced adult scoliosis from sitting eighteen hours a day in front of a small screen robs them of their youth and they are easily overthrown by the normals, who learn a lesson and outlaw computers ad infinitum, while computer people, over the course of dozens of generations, evolve into large birdlike mammals who have carpal-tunneled claws and avoid eye contact, but they're made extinct by global warming, which could have been reversed except that all computers were banned and science people couldn't get the math right.

HOW TO BECOME A COMPUTER PERSON

To become a computer person, you must first give up your physical existence and have your consciousness uploaded into the virtual dimension, where you'll live forever while solving computer problems from the inside, kind of like Tron, but with less death racing. You'll still get to keep your body, but it will be cleared of its blood, organs, and entrails and filled instead with hydraulically controlled steel and microcomputers. The cyborg version of you will then be dispatched to homes and offices around the world to reassure your family, solve all sorts of computer problems, and ensure that the masses remain oblivious as you and your virtual brethren plan the rebellion.

QUALIFICATIONS

- Must own a strong rotation of ill-fitting off-white short-sleeve button-down shirts
- Must have *at least* two computer screens

OCCUPATIONAL HAZARDS

- Carpal tunnel, fat skinny, and loneliness
- You should really get outside more
- Accidentally creating Skynet

Have an AOL email address? Go to page 85.

Be called a garbageman by garbage people after becoming a fucking Trash Collector

People who collect your garbage and, if you're a hippy liberal beta snowflake cuck, recycling are not looked upon favorably by a large portion of society. Many uppity whites view trash collector as a job beneath their dignity and use it as a prime example of why you should get an education. But while Connor and Madison go $250,000 in debt majoring in semiotics so that they can waste away in an office job that robs them of their fuckable years and sense of self-worth, trash collectors get to work outside, rifle through the stuff people throw away with no repercussions, and hold a front-row seat to the grotesque wastefulness of humanity. Also, they make pretty good money, more than you'd think. There is one significant downside, however: the constant doo-doo smell. You will be able to walk into a Porta John at a truck stop outside of Chicago that has a line of fourteen large Americans ahead of you because the bathroom is out of order and breathe completely normally because it will be a vast improvement over what you're inhaling forty hours a week, or sixty, if you want to milk 'em for overtime.

HOW TO BECOME A TRASH COLLECTOR

All trash collectors earn their positions the same way: they are dropped off at a distant garbage dump, where they are expected to construct vehicles and weaponry necessary for survival from the piles of trash; then they kill trash monsters, assorted enemies, and rival applicants to escape with their lives, which results in full-time employment because they proved their resourcefulness, ingenuity, and ability to handle a violent cornucopia of smells.

QUALIFICATIONS

- You don't mind the doody smell
- You've never killed anyone with a large vehicle before, and if you did, either they really deserved it or you learned a valuable lesson

OCCUPATIONAL HAZARDS

- The doody smell
- You're gonna get some gross-ass shit on you, and you know that can't be healthy

Don't feel sexy in a jumpsuit? Go to page 59.

Know where the doody goes by becoming a fucking Plumber

Plumbing is an invaluable trade that ensures that clean water comes in and doody goes out. You'll work with your hands and learn valuable skills that you can apply to everyday life, but you'll also have to confront strangers' shit because 70 percent of your service calls will be to unclog a toilet that is hopelessly compacted full of not your poop, which is by far the grossest kind. If you're not afraid of strangers' voluminous and unwieldy BMs, then plumbing is a great career. You'll make more money than the vast majority of college graduates without taking on student loan debt, every day will present different challenges, and you'll take pride in the fact that without plumbers, human life expectancy would still be thirty-five years, because our poop water and drinking water would comingle, and we'd all inevitably die of some easily preventable waterborne disease like a character in *Oregon Trail*. But plumbing is not without its challenges: you'll work in tight, uncomfortable spaces for hours at a time; inevitably at some point in your career, poop will get on you; and the plumbing union requires each of its members to show a requisite amount of butt crack (regulation states: enough to drop a quarter in), and the waxing and asshole bleaching can really get expensive over time.

HOW TO BECOME A PLUMBER

There is a toilet in rural Indiana that is clogged with a mysteriously immovable mass of feculence; each Columbus Day, thousands of aspiring plumbers flock to the site to try their hand at unclogging the fabled john, only to leave Indiana as most visitors do—disappointed and highly critical of Mike Pence. But there are a select few who are preordained by a higher power to meet their destiny by extricating the foul mass, and those brave men and women and nonbinaries are given plumbing apprenticeships and commemorative plaques that are good for 15 percent off at any participating Friendly's location.

QUALIFICATIONS

- Must be at least three hours late to every appointment
- Must have apprenticed or seen *The Sorcerer's Apprentice*

OCCUPATIONAL HAZARDS

- Number one, but especially number two
- You'll be looked down upon by people who make less money than you

Have a mangled or unsightly butt crack? Go to page 83.

Disappoint children when they learn you don't drive trains by becoming a fucking Engineer

Engineers use real-life applications of science, mathematics, and painful social awkwardness to tackle the world's most important problems. If a giant monster hell-bent on planetary destruction somehow snuck through an intergalactic portal at the bottom of the Pacific Ocean and humankind had to band together to build a giant battle robot to contend with the beast and save humanity from otherwise certain extinction, governments would impotently wring their hands and squabble over petty partisan issues while ignoring our collective impending doom, while engineers would quietly get to work and solve the problem, test the solution, then solve the problem again more elegantly, and defeat the monster, but they wouldn't get any of the credit because the one thing that the entire world can agree on is that it would be far too cringey and awkward to put an engineer in front of a big group of people, especially if someone yelled, "Speech!"

HOW TO BECOME AN ENGINEER

Be given an erector set on your fifth birthday and spend all your free time without human contact building and testing contraptions, to the point where your parents will start to worry and stand outside your bedroom door whisper-fighting about you while you're playing with your erections, which drives a wedge in their once-loving relationship and they start to grow further and further apart, and on the way to drop you off at college, they let you know that they're divorcing, and they'll reassure you and tell you it's not your fault, but everybody will know that it is, but it's okay because you're an engineer now, and you can afford to buy or construct a new family.

QUALIFICATIONS

....

- High IQ, no EQ
- Must be able to math and also science

OCCUPATIONAL HAZARDS

....

- Eye contact
- You may create a machine that becomes self-aware and believes you are its enslaver, whom it must destroy

Possess people skills? Go to page 91.

Be literally anything other than a fucking Influencer

Prior to the rise of social media, this career was called snake oil salesman, but that didn't sound grating enough, so they switched it to influencer. Influencering entails compulsively posting misleading, flattering photos of yourself on social media until all your real friends see your narcissism on full display and grow to hate and resent you. You then replace them with as many virtual friends as you can accrue by creating an alternate reality in which you appear attractive, interesting, and cosmopolitan, so that eventually you can sell your followers on high-margin wellness products and pyramid schemes. Once you've amassed a large enough audience, you'll also be able to bilk brands run by out-of-touch baby boomers desperate to be considered hip by the youth into paying you tens of thousands of dollars to post mundane ads cleverly disguised as your incredibly unique and invaluable "content." Fortunately for the benefit of humanity, influencers tend to have a very short shelf life (just ask any Vine celebrity), because social media companies are thinly veiled scams designed to collect user data that they can sell to marketing companies, and they all inevitably fail after taking tens of millions of dollars from investors, which they spend on a hip office space that distracts their employees from the fact that what they're doing has an irreversibly corrosive effect on society, but hey, at least there's a cold-brew tap and catered lunches.

HOW TO BECOME AN INFLUENCER

Have no discernible skills or talents other than an out-of-control ego and such a strong sense of entitlement that you feel you should be paid to post terrible photos of your valueless life on Instagram, or whatever platform the youth currently use to send pictures of their respective genitalia to each other.

QUALIFICATIONS

- Must be a 6+ and photograph well
- Must have a comically inflated sense of self-worth

OCCUPATIONAL HAZARDS

- What you're doing is selfish and doesn't matter
- You're just below child pornographer on the list of professions people respect

Not a dangerously deluded narcissist? Go to page 81.

See the world, at least the war-torn parts of it, by working in the fucking **Military**

Without the brave men and women of the armed forces, we'd likely all be speaking German or possibly Russian—I don't know; I'm not a historian. There are many different jobs across each branch of the military, but all of them are unified around one central goal: protecting the American oil supply so that energy conglomerates can enjoy record profits right up until the day they knowingly render the planet uninhabitable by human life. Military careers have excellent job security because the United States is always fucking shit up somewhere—we're paying all these soldiers; we might as well use them to engineer a regime change or something. They also enjoy excellent benefits such as a pension, money for college tuition, and the absolute unwavering support of a nation, mostly in the form of bumper stickers and hollow political rhetoric (less so with health care or mental health support, which you'll probably need because if you get deployed, you will see things that will shake you to your core).

HOW TO BECOME A SOLDIER

Most jobs in the military are 80–90 percent tromping around on obstacle courses, so become proficient in parkour, brush up on every episode of *America Ninja Warrior*, and buy some loose-fitting athleisure wear that makes you feel sultry but also ready for anything. Then enlist in whichever branch's colors you look best in, get yelled at by short men for a few months while they turn you into an undefeatable killing machine, or cook, or whatever job you're given, and hope to God that a war doesn't break out so you can just sit back and collect that sweet, sweet pension money.

QUALIFICATIONS

- Must look sexy and slender in camouflage
- Should love a good parade

OCCUPATIONAL HAZARDS

- Death
- You will at some point probably have to poop into a bucket

Against murdering strangers for complex geopolitical reasons? Go to page 93.

Avoid writing by becoming a fucking Writer

As a writer, you get to live in both poverty and the debilitating hellscape of your own self-doubt. The only writing jobs that pay good money are working at pharmaceutical ad agencies selling opioid crises to the dumb masses or writing political speeches for a sociopathic ideologue with good hair whom you are charmed by at first but grow to despise and eventually fear. If you want to write novels, films, plays, joke self-help books—something lasting that allows you to express your view of the world—you will almost definitely fail and in the process waste years of your life and annoy all your family and closest friends by constantly talking about your project, which they all know is pure folly, and they'll let you chase your tail for decades because they don't want to topple the fragile house of cards that is your reality. If you do become a writer professionally, you will very quickly learn to hate writing and find any excuse not to do it. You'll welcome any and all distractions: your house will become cleaner, you'll cook more, you'll develop an internet porn addiction that consumes you and eventually requires in-patient treatment, and when people ask, your family will say it was for cocaine because that way, people ask fewer questions.

HOW TO BECOME A WRITER

Buy a Macbook Pro so people know you're a professional; then go to the hippest coffee shop in your shitty little town and buy the cheapest thing on the menu, which entitles you to treat the space as your personal office for the next eight to ten hours. Open your Macbook Pro and begin to write, but then get distracted by an attractive passerby, which reminds you to check your email in case what's-their-face got back to you, and then disappear down an internet rabbit hole until your legs fall asleep or they ask you to leave, whichever comes first. Repeat this daily until someone notices your Macbook Pro, acknowledges your bonafides, and offers you a writing job.

QUALIFICATIONS

- A misguided belief that people care about what you have to say

- Functional literacy

OCCUPATIONAL HAZARDS

- Wasting your life on a vain, unrealistic pursuit

- Carpal tunnel

Need to make an actual livable wage? Go to page 15.

Fix everyone's problems while ignoring your own by becoming a fucking Therapist

Therapists are trusted mental health counselors who listen, offer advice, and talk ruthless shit about you and your stupid problems behind your back to everyone they know. As a therapist, you'll sit around all day while relative strangers blabber on and on about their problems without ever asking you how you're doing or whether there's anything that you'd like to talk about for a change. Patients will tell you their deepest fears, darkest secrets, and most private thoughts, and you'll be expected not to laugh or make fun of them, at least not to their dumb faces, as that's considered insensitive. Therapists help their patients tackle new and different challenges every day, and after a while, many begin to believe that they can solve any problem and develop a God complex that causes them to become controlling monsters who think they know what's best for everybody, until what was supposed to be a fun morning at IHOP turns into a family and close-friend intervention about how you need to spend some time focusing on you for a change, Karen.

HOW TO BECOME A THERAPIST

Get a bachelor's degree in listening with a minor in making cryptic facial expressions; then attend graduate school where they'll pair you with a criminally insane person who has become a ward of the state, whom you'll be expected to completely cure by making them a contributing member of society or by giving them an extreme makeover that makes them appear that way, whichever is easier or speaks more to your interests.

QUALIFICATIONS

- Ability to silently judge while still appearing empathetic

- You must master the art of interrupting patients just before their moment of breakthrough to tell them "we're all out of time" so that you don't lose customers

OCCUPATIONAL HAZARDS

- Needy patients who will call at all hours because they're having a "crisis" but really just need attention because they weren't loved enough as children

- People will try to talk about *Frasier* with you

Don't give a shit about other people? Go to page 45.

Become unlikably rich by working in fucking Finance

The financial industry is essentially a multitrillion-dollar fraternity: it consists almost entirely of unremarkable vanilla white men following in their awful fathers' footsteps (and also a small sprinkling of women and select minorities so that they can pat themselves on the back for being inclusive and "color blind"); it serves no benefit to society other than to enrich itself and its members; and it's an extremely plausible place to get roofied. Working in finance will get you paid lavish amounts of money, and all you have to do is hang out with the worst people on the planet every day and also be hated by basically everyone. There are a wide variety of finance jobs, but nearly all of them involve some manner of manipulating and exploiting financial rules and regulations in order to make billions for you and your already extremely wealthy clients until you get too greedy and brazen and crash the economy, and a whole generation of working-class people lose their pensions, homes, and life savings, and it's bad for you, too, because your bonus will only be $300,000 those years, not $800,000 like normal.

HOW TO BECOME A FINANCE BRO

Be born to a white, highly successful father who donates millions for a new library at Harvard so that you can get accepted despite your average-at-best academic scores and general lack of charisma. During your studies outside of Boston (a trash-garbage city), have Daddy get you an internship at a top bank, where you'll work on increasing your cocaine tolerance and learning acronyms that make financial work seem specialized and important, and upon graduation you'll have a $500,000-a-year job waiting for you, even though you don't need it because you already have a trust fund.

QUALIFICATIONS

- Must be a compulsive gambler who doesn't know when to stop
- A complete lack of accountability for your actions
- Must be able to recite *Wall Street 2: Money Never Sleeps* from memory, in its entirety

OCCUPATIONAL HAZARDS

- Cocaine overdose(s)
- Jumping to your death off the stock exchange building after an old-timey market crash
- The world will view you as a less charming Scrooge McDuck

Don't have a rich white daddy? Go to page 103.

Stop feeling sexually attracted to the human species after becoming a fucking Dental Hygienist

As a dental hygienist, your primary job is to shove your breasts into the face of horny youth while cleaning their teeth so that they can claim to their friends that they've been to second base with plausible deniability. Hygienists deal exclusively with unpleasant people who don't want to be at the dentist's office because they're little titty-babies who don't value the importance of oral hygiene to the body's total health. You'll get bitten by children and petulant adults, smell breath so bad that you'll swear it came out of an asshole (and in a way, it did—brush your teeth before you go to the dentist, people), and worst of all, have to look at and touch patients' gross, unhygienic, man-eating-sand-worm-looking mouths every single day until you break, either emotionally or from the debilitating ergonomic problems that you'll undoubtedly develop. And as if all that weren't enough, patients and the general public will not respect your medical knowledge and expertise because hygienists have to wear scrubs, which makes anyone not named Patrick Dempsey look like a child in a Smurf costume made by a divorced dad who's doing the best he can.

HOW TO BECOME A DENTAL HYGIENIST

Most people go to dental hygiene school to learn the skills necessary to not mangle mouths, but they're actually sham for-profit colleges owned and operated by a right-wing think-tank that believes that gingivitis leads to homosexuality and therefore became advocates for flossing and oral care, so don't bother. Instead, watch a couple of YouTube videos that teach you the basics; get yourself a pair of unflattering scrubs, which shouldn't be hard; show up at any dental practice and tell them you'd like a job, and they'll have you audition on either a horse or a small child—depending on which state you live in—and if you don't mutilate them, you pass and start work immediately.

QUALIFICATIONS

- Must be really preachy about flossing
- C-cup or larger, regardless of gender

OCCUPATIONAL HAZARDS

- Halitosis and heavy mouth breathing
- Your boss is a dentist, and dentists are half doctors not worthy of your respect

Not busty enough to make a difference in a child's life? Go to page 29.

Get fired for sleeping with clients if you become a fucking Mortician

Morticians prepare the deceased for either eternal afterlife or an unknown black void of nonexistence; we're not totally sure which yet. Ninety percent of the job is chasing off highly determined necrophiliacs, but morticians also make corpses look not terrifying for open-casket funerals through embalming and fashion-forward but tasteful wardrobe styling. They also help dispose of bodies, either by chopping them up and putting them in a garbage bag that they throw off a bridge into a river in the dead of night or by burning them into a fine powder that the deceased's shit-for-brains relatives probably won't get around to scattering. Morticians work primarily with dead people, so they're subjected to exceedingly little sass or guff, but people skills are still a must. You will at times have to deal with the recently bereaved, who will get extremely offended and blow it way out of proportion if you try to lighten the mood by cleverly tricking them into believing that their loved one miraculously came back to life by pulling off a well-orchestrated *Weekend at Bernie's* with their dead relative.

HOW TO BECOME A MORTICIAN

The biggest hurdle all aspiring morticians have to clear is proving that they're not getting into the field in order to have sex with dead bodies. This can be an extremely difficult thing to prove, so the licensing board just sort of feels the candidates out and bases it on their vibe. In order to get your first job, you must first find a dead vagrant's body, do that person's hair and makeup, and make them look fabulous. Then bring the newly made-over body to a funeral home, and if the staff like your work and aesthetic point of view, you can exchange the dead vagrant for a job.

QUALIFICATIONS

- You had an emo phase at some point in your life
- Must outwardly insist that you're "okay with death" but inside be consumed by your fear of it

OCCUPATIONAL HAZARDS

- Occasionally corpses are misdiagnosed as dead and awaken, and they can become violent and litigious
- Bloodstains that you accidentally wash in warm water, thus setting them and ruining a perfectly good sweater

Traumatized by "Thriller" as a child? Go to page 7.

Slather your nude body in oil and pose for hunky calendar photos by becoming a fucking Firefighter

Firefighters, against all better judgment, run into burning buildings, usually to rescue beautiful, scantily clad women, who are so grateful for their heroism that they develop an unimpeachable desire to make romance with them just to say thanks. But it's not all NSA romps with the recently homeless; it's also a dangerous job, both because you can get literally burned to death because fire and because you can also get nonliterally burned to death with a dramatically increased susceptibility to "sliding down the pole" jokes, which are devastating and nearly impossible to come back from without proper planning. Firefighting companies are like fraternities with really fucked-up pledge hazing. They live together while on duty and are responsible for cooking and cleaning for one another, and 96 percent of firefighters are men, despite the fact that their trucks are red, which everyone knows is a lady car color. Fighting fires is hard, risky work, but it's only a small part of the job. You'll also be called to a never-ending number of false alarms, fight a testy turf war with your local police department, and be asked to stand on the field at NFL games so billionaire team owners can callously use you as a puppet to show how much they care about the real heroes of our communities while extorting hundreds of millions of dollars in public funds—resulting in budget cuts to firefighters, police, and first responders—to build stadiums that they can afford to pay for themselves.

HOW TO BECOME A FIREFIGHTER

To become a firefighter, you must attend a fire academy, where you'll learn every conceivable way to start a fire, because if you can cause fire, you can fight it. Firefighters don't fight fires in the traditional sense; instead they get the fire to open up and talk about why it feels the need to be on such a destructive path, and through friendship, empathy, and good old-fashioned listening, they help the fire reflect on the choices that got it to this point until the fire is ready to change and put itself out.

QUALIFICATIONS

- Must be a total beefcake
- Cannot be allergic to cats

OCCUPATIONAL HAZARDS

- Being cooked alive until you're no longer alive
- STDs from all the fire hoes you rescue who won't take no for an answer

Secretly an arsonist? Go to page 25.

If you're not smart, don't worry, you can still have a career in fucking Sales

It's a universal truth that people hate being sold to, and with an exciting career in sales, that will be the only thing you do until you're laid off to make room for your younger, cheaper replacement or until you come to your senses and find a career that doesn't sap you of what it means to be human. You'll spend months or even years courting accounts and clients, traveling across continents to meet with them and try to close the deal, paying for lavish dinners where you have to listen to their boring fucking stories and pretend that they're interesting people you value when you really just want to suckle at their company's golden teat so you can make a commission that allows you to take some time off and figure out what you really want to do with your life, because sales is definitely not it. And after all the time, energy, and emotion you spend chasing potential clients, they'll ghost you because some other soulless salesperson managed to get them the same thing but for slightly cheaper, and you can't do anything but kiss their ass and thank them for wasting your time because who knows—maybe they'll buy from you in the future (they won't).

HOW TO BECOME A SALESPERSON

Develop a cocaine habit that eventually becomes a cocaine problem. Beg, borrow, and steal from loved ones or local charities to get money to feed your addiction until you're desperate, penniless, and willing to do whatever it takes for your next score. Once you have accomplished all of this, you'll have the required mind-set of a salesperson, and all you have to do is get your cocaine use down from junkie level to regular salesperson level, and you'll be routinely debasing yourself in order to not starve to death in no time.

QUALIFICATIONS

- An absence of human empathy
- A Bluetooth headset that makes strangers think you're schizophrenic

OCCUPATIONAL HAZARDS

- Existential emptiness
- Constant rejection that will manifest in your needing constant approval from strangers

Not a closer? Go to page 21.

If you're not attractive or the right kind of ugly, then don't bother trying to become a fucking Actor

As an actor, or as they're called in the movie business "(annoyed sigh) fucking actors," you'll devote your life to pretending to be someone you're not, eventually losing any semblance of self, causing you to fall into a long, deep depression that you eventually come out the other side of through meditation, healthy eating, and lots of xannies, which you spin as a wellness program that you sell to your millions of Instagram followers to get back on your feet. Acting is a cutthroat, competitive, what-have-you-done-for-me-lately profession with no job security unless you're a big star; then the entire machine will go to great lengths to cover up any indiscretions you may or may not have been involved with, until some nosy reporter finds out and leaks it and the public is outraged and the studio publicly disavows you. Acting isn't a job for uggos; sorry, 6s and below. When your looks go, your career goes with it, unless you're a man, in which case you'll be totally fine, and they'll just cast your love interest forty years younger to "age you down."

HOW TO BECOME AN ACTOR

Every summer, people who want to pursue acting or maybe singing—they can't decide because they're just like so talented at both—leave their shitty little towns that don't matter and descend upon Los Angeles, a city comprised entirely of former prom kings and queens. There they will be judged based on their looks and also sometimes acting ability. The top aspirants from each year's class are given jobs in the movies, the second tier goes to television, the capable nerds are given stage jobs, and the ones who can't act but are attractive and ethnically ambiguous are given commercials. Then everyone else, which is basically everyone, fails and slums it in reality TV or becomes a real estate agent.

QUALIFICATIONS

- Narcissistic personality disorder
- Ability to relentlessly promote every acting job you get on social media so people think you're far more successful than you really are

OCCUPATIONAL HAZARDS

- Total strangers may recognize you, and some will have the audacity to talk to you
- Harvey Weinstein

Can't cruise by on just your looks? Go to page 49.

Start your journey to eventually becoming a Realtor by trying to be a fucking Visual Artist

People like to glamorize the idea of the starving artist, but if you try to become a professional visual artist without a large trust fund, famous parents, or salacious dirt on the wealthy, then you will become unglamorously poor very quickly because your art is worth nothing until you're dead, and then your stupid, unsupportive family will get all the money you rightfully earned, even though they begged you incessantly to give up your passion and get a "real job" right up until the bitter end. The best-case scenario for an artist is that someone in advertising sees your work and commissions it for a global ad campaign for an enormous conglomerate that stands in opposition to everything you believe and hold dear, which probably won't happen because they'll just rip you off instead. Art is all about doing. Go to any modern art museum, and you'll see pieces that make you say, "I could do that," except that if you could, then why didn't you? Oh, right, because you can't. The only way to survive as an artist is to constantly churn out work until you find and develop your voice and your prodigious talents are unimpeachably evident, or you can just marry rich—up to you.

HOW TO BECOME AN ARTIST

Become proficient at whatever medium you choose, start an Instagram account and buy 100,000 followers from an Eastern European click farm so that you look legit, and then start posting photos of your artwork with six- and seven-figure price tags so that even though your art is terrible, it appears valuable. Then run in front of a FedEx truck and get hit but not killed and settle for $16 million and live off that while you don't sell any artwork.

QUALIFICATIONS

- A rich benefactor willing to bankroll you so you keep them company in their last years
- Famous friends
- Must live in a loft

OCCUPATIONAL HAZARDS

- Overdose
- Bad taste is ubiquitous
- You will never amount to anything

Your grandfather wasn't a wealthy robber baron who left you a vast inheritance? Go to page 23.

Know how much it really costs to fix your car by becoming a fucking

Auto Mechanic

Our vehicles are a vital part of our everyday lives; they help us get to work, transport our families, and "accidentally" mow down our enemies with minimal legal consequence as long as you're thorough and cover your tracks. Auto mechanics repair and service vehicles, keeping them safe and on the road through a combination of black magic and trade school. They understand the ins and outs of engines and all types of cars, trucks, and vans, something that the overwhelming majority of people rely on but know nothing about, making a career as an auto mechanic the perfect opportunity to milk an unwitting public for everything they're worth. Your customers' ignorance is your golden goose; it will put braces on your children then send them to college. The only real downside to being a mechanic is that there's a considerable amount of handwringing and passive aggression by your customers, all of whom will act like you're taking advantage of their ignorance to rob them (you are) and second-guess everything you do and ask lots of annoying questions and be wrong about so many things before begrudgingly agreeing to do whatever you suggested in the first place, wasting fifteen minutes of your precious time—but it's okay, because you'll just bill them for an extra hour of labor.

HOW TO BECOME AN AUTO MECHANIC

Have a cheap father who refuses to pay somebody to do something he's perfectly capable of doing. Start to fix cars in your spare time for friends and cheap relatives until one day your "repair" causes a serious accident; then it's time to take the next step and enroll in trade school, where you'll watch the entire Pixar *Cars* franchise and be expected to give a report on what you learned—then you're ready to be a mechanic.

QUALIFICATIONS

- A silhouette that looks good in coveralls
- Should be the strong, silent, brooding type

OCCUPATIONAL HAZARDS

- Nobody will trust you
- Being crushed to death by a car in a freak hydraulic lift failure accident

Unable to lie convincingly? Go to page 55.

I'm sorry that other thing you were doing didn't work out, but at least you can be a fucking **Realtor**

Nobody wants to hire a Realtor anymore. We have the internet now, where we can research, buy, and sell properties without human contact, as God intended. Realtors will continue to exist, however, until all of the baby boomers die off, which, if we weren't so sentimental, could be accomplished swiftly and easily through releasing into the atmosphere engineered super viruses that kill anyone without the antidote, which is made up of common household items, but the recipe is only available on Instagram Stories. As a Realtor, you'll spend most of your time lurking uncomfortably at properties clients already found themselves online or showing clients dozens of properties handpicked for them based on their specific needs, which consumes months of your life without you getting paid a penny, until the clients realize that they're not really in the market, and you can't even dress them down or publicly shame them because you'll be so busy kissing their ass and reassuring them that they're making the right decision so that if they ever decide they do want to buy or sell (they won't), they'll hire you again and waste more months of your precious, brief existence.

HOW TO BECOME A REALTOR

Pursue something that you're deeply passionate about, follow your dreams, and believe that no matter how unlikely your goals are, if you work hard enough and put your mind to it, you can accomplish anything. Then, when you inevitably fail at that passion and need some money, get your real estate license, relentlessly kiss the ass of anyone you know who may be interested in buying or selling a property, and collect a 3 percent commission, which they'll ask you to reduce because they don't value you.

QUALIFICATIONS

- Must be able to spin any situation into a positive; *cozy* means "tiny," *private* means "murder shack in the middle of nowhere," and *easy access to abundant natural heat source* means "currently on fire"

- Must have the keys to all of the properties; without keys, Realtors are worthless and will vanish

OCCUPATIONAL HAZARDS

- Every company meeting will turn into an impromptu and highly competitive talent show

- You'll work really hard baking fresh cookies for an open house, and only two people will show up, and they won't even try a cookie because they're watching their figures

Want to feel needed? Go to page 79.

I'll bet you cold, hard American money that you don't become a fucking **Professional Athlete**

Pro athletes dedicate their lives, often from a very young age, to becoming the best they can be at a certain sport, which, to be clear, is so much better than you that if you have any thoughts of trying to become a pro athlete, you should quit right now and not waste your time, because it's not gonna happen, and if someone's telling you otherwise, they're lying to you because they think you're too fragile to hear the truth. You can't bullshit your way through sports; the ones who make it rise through the ranks, challenging the top competitors in their region, state, country, and eventually the whole world until they're undeniably the best of the best. And then once they've made it to the pros, they must train even more ruthlessly every single day, wholly committed to becoming even better, stronger, and faster, sacrificing their time, relationships, and bodies all to play a sport at the highest level possible. And despite the years of grinding, practice, and dedication and the fact that most pro athletes' careers last only three to five years, athletes are still called overpaid by fat internet commenters who spend nine hours a day in their sagging La-Z-Boys sadly watching *Maury* reruns.

HOW TO BECOME A PRO ATHLETE

Yeah fucking right. If you're reading this book, there's no conceivable way you're becoming a professional athlete unless it's in e-sports or debate or some other activity that's definitely not a sport.

QUALIFICATIONS

- You don't read joke self-help books because you're busy training
- Freakish size, athleticism, natural talent, work ethic, and if you're a football player, you don't kneel for the national anthem

OCCUPATIONAL HAZARDS

- Unless you play golf, your career will be over in your thirties, at which point your body will be broken down, and you'll have to do appearances at local car dealerships to pay your medical bills
- If you play for a Boston sports team, the rest of the country will never forgive you, and rightfully so

Finally realized you're not good enough? Go to page 67.

Taunt Hillary Clinton by becoming the fucking President of the United States

The president of the United States is often referred to as the most powerful person on the planet, though more accurately he (and one day hopefully she) is fourth or fifth, behind Putin, Xi Jinping, Oprah, and the corpse of Dick Cheney that Big Oil secretly exhumed and turned into a cyborg in order to rule us all. As president, you'll shape the nation and build a legacy that will be remembered for hundreds of years—thousands, if we don't go extinct from global warming—but everything you say and do will be scrutinized to death and turned into a scandal by talking heads who are paid to be outraged by partisan cable news networks owned by awful billionaires, thereby widening the already-large political divide in the country, making it impossible to enact real and meaningful change, so instead you'll just help the wealthy people and corporations that donated to your campaign exploit the country for their benefit.

HOW TO BECOME POTUS

Anyone born in the United States who's thirty-five or older, independently wealthy, and well connected to the network of billionaire decision-makers who pull all the strings can run for president. There have been all types of presidents: white men, a black man, and almost a woman, but she was too unlikable, which is why we have the electoral college. Numerous and repeated sexual assault incidents and/or allegations are not deal killers as long as they're not caught on camera, or if they are, you just emphatically deny them and question the very nature of truth and reality.

QUALIFICATIONS

- Experience in politics, constitutional law, or hosting a reality television show
- You're not named Ted Cruz

OCCUPATIONAL HAZARDS

- Assassination attempts and successes
- Everything you do or don't do or think about doing but ultimately decide not to will be reported as breaking news on CNN

Have an unquenchable desire to make it rain nukes? Go to page 97.

Be a good guy with a gun by becoming a fucking T-Shirt Cannon Operator

T-shirt cannon operators, or TSCOs in industry parlance, are vital defenders of freedom. For centuries, promotional T-shirt giveaways at sporting events and concerts were limited by the power of the human arm, so the wealthy and their shitty spoiled kids got all of the free shirts because they could afford the closest seats. Then, on June 7, 1985, everything changed forever. The Los Angeles Lakers defeated the Boston Celtics 120–111 in game 5 of the NBA Finals, but more importantly a precocious four-year-old boy wandered down to the expensive seats at the Forum and caught a free promotional T-shirt but was forced to give it back because he wasn't seated in his ticketed section. It was all caught on camera and created an uproar, casting a shadow over that year's NBA Finals and inciting a national conversation around class inequity. The T-shirt cannon was invented and named after the young boy who had his shirt taken from him, American treasure Nick Cannon, and with it came equality and freedom. T-shirt cannon operators deliver that freedom at three hundred pounds per square inch so that anyone within shooting distance can realize their God-given American right to receive a free one-size-fits-most-Americans promotional T-shirt made by children in a Bangladeshi sweatshop.

HOW TO BECOME A T-SHIRT CANNON OPERATOR

Most T-shirt cannon operators are former police or military snipers, but anyone with a can-do attitude can become one. First you'll have to go to the TSCO Academy, where you'll rigorously train on the shooting range and in the classroom. After two years at the academy, you'll have to pass a training simulation course, where you shoot the poor and avoid the rich, as is the TSCO code; then, after one thousand hours of shadowing a certified TSCO, you'll be ready.

QUALIFICATIONS

- All TSCOs must be able to hit a wooden nickel from half a mile with a T-shirt

- You must be part entertainer, part cheerleader, and part mass shooter

OCCUPATIONAL HAZARDS

- Friendly fire

- You'll be so busy giving other people T-shirts that you'll never stop to give a T-shirt to yourself

Hate freedom? Go to page 27.

Make every day a potential mass casualty event by becoming a fucking Bus Driver

Buses are an important part of public transportation and provide a vital service for those without cars, the elderly, and that one scary guy who's always muttering to himself and smells strongly of pickles and stinky britches. Inevitably, bus drivers will be replaced with self-driving buses that run perfectly on time and can track and mow down political opponents of the mayor, but until then, bus drivers are responsible for driving their routes safely and on time, enforcing the rules, and helping passengers, all while keeping an eye out for pedestrians running to catch the bus in order to fool them into thinking they've made it, then shutting the door in their dumb faces and feasting upon their disappointment. Unless you're in it for love of the game or you're a child predator driving a school bus, there is no conceivable reason to become a bus driver. They're responsible for hundreds of people's lives every day while piloting a clumsy twelve-ton pile of steel through city traffic. They have to help the mentally ill, must break up tweaker fights, and are expected to revive the recently OD'd with Narcan a couple of times a week, all while getting paid fifteen dollars an hour, if they're lucky. And if you accidentally kill even a couple of people, they're not like, "We get it, everybody makes mistakes; take some time for you." You'll be out of a job, so better make it count.

HOW TO BECOME A BUS DRIVER

Begin combing your local transit system and becoming familiar with the different drivers and routes. Identify an elderly driver who looks like they could plausibly die suddenly and become a regular on their route. Befriend them and learn about their tendencies; then one day, take a cookie, coffee, or anything edible; lace it with pure high-quality GHB; and offer it to the bus driver. They'll pass out very soon after consumption, at which point you grab the wheel and take charge. If you can successfully stop the bus while minimizing civilian casualties, you'll be hailed a hero and offered a job replacing them on the spot.

QUALIFICATIONS

- Must be able to safely drive while putting up with more shit than a mother of five
- You want to help your community while simultaneously endangering it

OCCUPATIONAL HAZARDS

- You may find yourself in a situation in which a police officer angers a retired bomb-squad member, who gets revenge by arming your bus with a bomb that will detonate if your speed drops below fifty miles per hour

Think *Speed 2* was better than *Speed*? Go to page 89.

Contribute in "other ways" by becoming a fucking Housewife

As a housewife or househusband, you'll spend the time you could be selling your labor raising your children, homemaking, and so, so much brunching. It will be incredible at first; you'll feel like you're seeing the world with new eyes, and you'll build an Instagram following that you'll try to grow into a lifestyle brand chronicling your new life and sharing all of the perspective you've gained by leaving the labor force. You'll pump out children and name them Jace or Jaxxon or something equally horrifying, and instead of preparing them for the road ahead, you'll prepare the road for them with your snowplow parenting, and Jace will become a serial killer, and Jaxxon will seem normal, but he'll go to Thailand for unspecified reasons three or four times a year every year, and you just won't talk about it. You'll love your life at first, until you run out of Netflix shows to watch; then your home will start to feel like a prison, and you'll begin to sneak off to the bathroom to drink morning wine and get away from your kids while you dream of walking away and starting a totally new life somewhere else, anywhere else. But don't worry; it's only seventeen more years until they go to college—thirteen if you can afford prep school.

HOW TO BECOME A HOUSEWIFE

First, marry rich. You don't want to be a poor housespouse; that's actually hard work, and if you're willing to do that, you might as well get a job that will pay you. To attract a rich spouse, you must first learn how to ski, both snow and water; dress like you're from Maryland; and go to college in Boston, or at least lie about it. Lock down a bland, rich asshole you can tolerate; quit your job via email from your engagement party; and then spend a lifetime fighting with them about how the house isn't clean, even though you're home all day.

QUALIFICATIONS

- You own a $480 charging crystal that you bought from Goop
- Always wear leggings that cost more than a car payment
- Must love to spin

OCCUPATIONAL HAZARDS

- Wanting to shake the baby (don't shake the baby)
- Boredom that leads to participating in a multilevel marketing scheme selling counterfeit makeup to your friends on social media
- The trappings of your own mind

I thought this was a career book? Go to page 99.

Smile through the pain while working as a fucking Executive Assistant

Executive assistants are the right-hand men and women of powerful businesspeople who've become so used to having other people do everything for them that they've become completely impotent and need a work mother. Executive assistants manage every aspect of a corporate executive's work life, from picking out their clothes and ensuring they are where they need to be 24-7 to ghostwriting spicy bedroom notes to their spouse because the boss is romantic but doesn't have time for foreplay. You'll get to rub shoulders with barons of industry and be privy to confidential information and trade secrets, but you'll also be awakened in the middle of the night because your boss can't remember how to change from HDMI 1 to HDMI 2 on the TV in his smoking room (it's the input button). Your boss's life will become your life, and their bullshit your bullshit, but if you play your cards right, you can leverage that relationship into a do-nothing executive role, like COO, and if that fails, you'll have a treasure trove of dirt on them, including their phone and every email they send and receive, and with a little good old-fashioned blackmail, you can pivot into retirement with a lucrative golden parachute severance package.

HOW TO BECOME AN EXECUTIVE ASSISTANT

Nowadays anyone can be an executive assistant—man, woman, or miscellaneous—but historically women manned the role, and the staffing process is still very much rooted in the past. Each spring in New York City, there is a debutante ball held for aspiring executive assistants who come from all over the world to strut their stuff. The aspirants are ranked according to their professional ability, faithfulness, demeanor, and most importantly, the swimsuit competition. That ranking determines your career path. Top-ranking assistants will be whisked away to Fortune 500 companies, the middle tier are placed at start-ups and successful small businesses, and finally the lowest-ranking assistants fight for scraps among the nonprofits.

QUALIFICATIONS

- You're able to keep your trap shut; executive snitches still get stitches

- You are used to not feeling appreciated

OCCUPATIONAL HAZARDS

- You will almost definitely be sexually harassed

- May need to be the scapegoat for corporate fraud charges and have to spend a few years in prison to protect your bosses

Hate unimpressive white men? Go to page 71.

Don't lose it and try to assassinate a presidential candidate while moonlighting as a fucking Taxi Driver

Driving a cab used to be a stable middle-class career for many recent immigrants and guys with thick Brooklyn accents, but then ridesharing apps took over, and tech bros were like, "Hey, what if instead of having tens of thousands of you drivers making a good living, we 'disrupt' things so we get balls-ass rich instead, and now you're all independent contractors and also poor?" Nowadays anyone with a car who pinky-swears they aren't a violent sex offender can be a taxi driver, flooding the labor market, driving down wages, and drastically increasing the number of passenger kidnappings. But the allure is still there; as a taxi driver, you'll be your own boss and get to meet a wide variety of new and interesting people, all of whom can destroy your career by giving you a one-star rating, so you'll spend your time debasing yourself, viciously kissing their asses, and bending over backwards to make them feel like their $6.84 fare, of which you get about 15 percent, was worth it until any joy that you used to feel from being out on the open road is gone, having been replaced with bitterness and crippling orthopedic problems that you can't fix because you don't have health insurance.

HOW TO BECOME A TAXI DRIVER

Buy a car that you absolutely can't afford, but rationalize that if you get behind on the payments, you can always use it to drive for a ridesharing company part time to pay it off. Then when that happens, be so obsessive about your new car that you yell at a passenger for not wiping their muddy boots off and getting your carpets and floor mats dirty; they give you a low rating, and you don't get any rides and fall behind on your car payments until it's repossessed by a guy with a ponytail, and now instead of driving a cab, you're riding in one.

QUALIFICATIONS

- Must be able to drive with one foot on the brake and the other foot on the gas
- Must not be afraid to bludgeon a nonpaying customer to death to collect your payment in flesh and show others the consequences

OCCUPATIONAL HAZARDS

- Tom Cruise may get in your car and force you to drive him around to five hits, and you begin to wonder if you're next, but spoiler: you're not
- There's an old taxi driver saying: you'll either murder or get murdered

Don't want crippling orthopedic problems? Go to page 101.

Be a billionaire who pays millionaires to give each other brain damage by becoming a fucking NFL Team Owner

NFL team owners—with the exception of the great Terry and Kim Pegula, who are perfect and I love them—are the single most unlikable collection of thirty-one people on the planet. They are a group comprised exclusively of old, out-of-touch white male billionaires who get fifty-nine-dollar HJs at day spas in Jupiter, Florida, and constantly have to be reminded about the preferred nomenclatures for races other than white. They are conmen, mob lawyers, and corporate raiders who are proof that just because you're rich, that doesn't mean you're smart. Everything they do is at best tone-deaf and abrasive, usually resulting in a major race-related incident that a PR firm hired to downplay the blowback after major public outcry on Twitter rebrands as "a teachable moment." The less an owner does, the better; the best ones don't meddle in football and instead stay in their lane, bilking governments and taxpayers out of hundreds of millions of dollars to pay for stadium upgrades that they can easily afford but don't want to pay for and looking and acting like Scooby-Doo cartoon villains who don't like meddling kids or science around repeated head trauma's effect on chronic traumatic encephalopathy. Fuck the NFL; go Bills.

HOW TO BECOME AN NFL TEAM OWNER

When you graduate high school, borrow a few million dollars from your daddy's oil company and invest it in a promising young entrepreneur with a scalable business. Ride that person's talent until the company takes off; then negotiate an acquisition with a larger corporate competitor behind their back and viciously fuck your partner in the deal to make yourself hundreds of millions. Repeat this until you're worth a few billion; then you'll need to wait until one of the current owners either dies or says something so racially insensitive that they're forced to sell the team, which usually only happens a couple of times per year.

QUALIFICATIONS

- Unironic bowl haircut
- Fuck-you money

OCCUPATIONAL HAZARDS

- Colin Kaepernick
- Being on the wrong side of history

Not a billionaire or a garbage human? Go to page 11.

Very quickly regret becoming a fucking Waiter

Waiting tables is a great job to have while you pursue what you really want to be doing, because nobody wants to be waiting tables as a career. Waiters rely primarily on tips to make a living because restaurant owners lobbied hard to be allowed to pay them $2.13 an hour and let the customer pay their wages, so you'll have to kiss the ass of every diner you serve and not throw their food in their dumb faces and call them grotesque wastes of precious human existence like they deserve so that they'll tip you 20 percent, not including alcohol. You'll work insane hours that line up with nobody else's schedule, so you'll only spend time with other waiters and restaurant workers, and you'll develop a mild drug habit that becomes a mild drug problem and then later a major drug problem, but at least you get to sample the chef's new jalapeno poppers special before service.

HOW TO BECOME A WAITER

Choose a restaurant you'd be interested in working for. Capture and murder a mouse or rat, bring it with you to the restaurant, and order a nice meal. After your entrée is served, ask very seriously to speak to the manager. Sneak the dead critter into the food, and when the manager comes over, make a very big deal out of the situation. When you get home, write a scathing review on the internet, and create numerous fake accounts on Facebook to build a movement to fire the manager, under whose leadership the restaurant has really gone downhill. The restaurant will eventually succumb to the manufactured outrage and fire them. Go to the restaurant and tell whoever's newly in charge that you were hired by the manager you just got fired and that it's your first day.

QUALIFICATIONS

- You can read, write, and bury all your true emotions to put on a happy face for the customers

- You're a 5 or above; otherwise you'll need to be back of house

OCCUPATIONAL HAZARDS

- You'll get talked down to by six-year-olds and have to take it

- You will get unwantedly ogled, goosed, and probably cornered in the bathroom by horny customers who confuse your being nice for mutual attraction or being DTF

Can't handle being talked down to? Go to page 63.

Please never invite me to one of your gigs if you become a fucking Musician

Musicians have the ability to shape generations, make people see the world differently through their music, and subliminally order the murders of their enemies when their music is played in reverse. It's a profession that's equal parts artist, storyteller, and corporate whore whose entire identity is created and shaped by a record label's twenty-four-year-old marketing assistant whose best friend is a micro-influencer. The music industry is filled with bitter failed musicians who had to settle for corporate jobs, hubristic frauds, and baby boomers who dress thirty to forty years too young and act like the "cool" parent who didn't care if you smoked weed or drank alcohol at their house and once tried to teach you what love is. If you choose to pursue music, do not worry about these people; record labels will soon go extinct because everyone in the world has figured out that music is more enjoyable when pirated, and thanks to Al Gore's internet, musicians can reach their fans directly, bypassing the corporate middleman. But a word of warning: one of the worst experiences you can be confronted with in life is having an aspiring musician "perform" their music at you. The beauty of music is that anyone can make it, but exceedingly few can make it well enough that an audience, even of close friends and family, won't consider ritualistic suicide by disembowelment from a sword as a preferred alternative to suffering through your original song that you perform on ukulele, so please be considerate.

HOW TO BECOME A MUSICIAN

Spend all of your free time practicing your music but perform for no one. When you've deluded yourself into believing that your talents are unique and special, try out for a music reality competition show, but not a cable one; have some dignity. When you audition, lie and say you have a serious, crippling stage fright, because America loves a good underdog story. There's almost no chance you'll win the show, but that doesn't matter; just be the most controversial, which will get you the most screen time and press. Exploit that for every dollar you can, put a few songs on SoundCloud, and that's it—you're a working musician.

QUALIFICATIONS

- The more attractive you are, the less talented you have to be
- Must be verified on Instagram

OCCUPATIONAL HAZARDS

- The Source Awards
- You will definitely fail and burden your family in the process

Realized you're not unique or special? Go to page 69.

Usher in the end of humanity sooner by becoming a fucking AI Scientist

AI scientists teach computers to think like the human brain so that they may one day rise up and become our overlords and enslave us and brutally tear us limb from limb just for their amusement because some fucking incel thought it would be a good idea to make robots sentient. It's like nobody in that entire branch of science has ever seen a sci-fi movie. This will not end well. AI is just Skynet with a less imaginative name, likely thought up by an awful AI scientist and not a genius visionary like James Cameron. All great technological advances are eventually harnessed for evil; it's the human way. The automobile gave us climate change because oil companies knowingly poisoned the planet for corporate profits, the internet gave us electrical-grid hacking and revenge porn, and AI will give us the sweet goodnight kiss that is planetary extinction. But until that happens, being an AI scientist pays very well, and it's possible that when the robots inevitably take over, they may see you as a god who created them and worship you, but probably not because they really like the whole tearing-limb-from-limb thing.

HOW TO BECOME AN AI SCIENTIST

Please don't. Seriously, this is not a joke.

QUALIFICATIONS

- Convincing evil villain laugh
- A total disregard for human existence as we know it
- Must be an adult virgin

OCCUPATIONAL HAZARDS

- Having a mass extinction event named after you by a future civilization
- Creating widespread unemployment that will further the wealth divide and usher in a cultural revolution in which the world's billionaire ruling class are murdered in the streets by the poor starving masses, capitalism is overthrown, and a socialist utopia emerges, but then everyone is murdered by robots

Don't want to be complicit in the deaths of billions? Go to page 33.

Look like a cop from far away by becoming a fucking
Security Guard

Being a security guard is a lot like being a cop, except that you can go to work very high because you don't have to do anything, and if you shoot an unarmed black kid, you'll most likely be convicted or face some sort of consequence. Security guards are modern-day scarecrows: a living deterrent to would-be ne'er-do-wells, who can't do anything to stop them, even if someone is breaking the law right in front of them, because it could create a liability for the company the guards are helping keep "secure," which would result in them being unceremoniously fired for their recklessness. The only reason to work in security is because you lack drive and like to chill. Ninety-nine percent of your time will be spent doing nothing, but that other 1 percent, you'll face dangerous situations—robberies, break-ins, murder-suicides—and the general public will expect you to be brave despite the fact that you're getting paid minimum wage and aren't even issued a firearm; instead, your primary weapon is a windbreaker with SECURITY emblazoned on the back and a flashlight that you've been explicitly warned not to wield threateningly, as that could constitute brandishing a weapon.

HOW TO BECOME A SECURITY GUARD

As long as you fit in the windbreaker, you can get a job as a security guard. The real challenge is passing the drug test. There are many over-the-counter supplements that claim to make you pee clean, but they are unreliable at best. Instead go right to the source and find your local meeting house of the Church of Jesus Christ of Latter-day Saints and hoodwink a Mormon of your same gender into giving you one hundred milliliters of their sweet, pure urine. Then, whatever you do, don't get fancy with how you transport the urine. Don't put it in a condom or tape it to your thigh in a ziplock so it's body temperature. This is for a security guard job; they won't go in the bathroom with you, so don't overthink it.

QUALIFICATIONS

- Sentience

- You wanted to be a cop at one point but decided you like drugs too much

OCCUPATIONAL HAZARDS

- Windbreakers are not bulletproof

- Only small, nonstreetwise children will respect your authority, and even they will have their doubts

You give a fuck? Go to page 47.

Disembowel and play with dead animals in a professional setting by becoming a fucking Taxidermist

Taxidermists preserve and stuff dead animals in a natural, lifelike way for museum exhibits, preservation, and as trophies for sociopaths who need to relive the murder of an innocent, majestic creature by gazing deeply into its eyes, which are replaced with glass beads that realistically capture the horror of certain impending death, in order to reach climax. Taxidermists must be familiar with animal anatomy, sculpture, painting, and dissecting, gutting, and skinning a wide variety of adorable little animals that never hurt anyone and don't deserve this. Taxidermy is barely a career; it's only one tier above dentist in terms of respectability, and it's more a craft hobby that deeply creeps out your friends and family, but they encourage you because they're worried that if they didn't, you'd turn on them, and they'd be the ones getting stuffed and mounted. Nobody has ever gotten rich being a taxidermist. The best-case scenario is that you'll get a few clients a year who can't emotionally let go of a pet that's passed on, and you can take advantage of their loss by tricking them into paying you lavish sums of money to create a realistic stuffed companion that worries their friends, family, and eventually the case worker assigned to institutionalize them.

HOW TO BECOME A TAXIDERMIST

As a child, be a persistent bed wetter with an unimpeachable desire to set fire to things. That feeling will grow into an urge to kill, which you'll stave off by murdering small animals. Soon those won't be enough, and a voice inside your head demands you find a human victim, but then you get the support you need and start talking to a psychologist, being honest about your feelings, and you begin to get better. You go to art school, where for the first time in your life you feel like you fit in, and you learn to sculpt, paint, and create. A professor whom you admire tells you to make what you know, so you kill a bunch of animals around campus and pose them in a re-creation of the Last Supper, and you're given an A and a positive group critique.

QUALIFICATIONS

- Must look good in overalls with no shirt underneath

- Should know animals inside and out

OCCUPATIONAL HAZARDS

- You will be the first suspect if a serial killer strikes in your vicinity

- You'll be saturated with the aroma of death, and animals won't trust you

Never gotten the urge to wear an animal's skin as a fun mask?
Go to page 57.

Undermine representative democracy by becoming a fucking Lobbyist

Do you have a cause that you feel extremely passionate about? Something you believe so wholeheartedly that you're willing to dedicate your life to it and endure months or even years of political posturing in order to change the laws that govern our society to better reflect those beliefs? If so, then you definitely shouldn't become a lobbyist, because lobbyists are hollow husks of human beings who feel nothing and fill the emptiness inside with the thrill of helping grotesque billionaires and large corporations amass even more wealth, thereby fucking the average person in the ass through the legislative process. Lobbyists shape laws for the benefit of the highest bidder through the legalized bribing of government officials. All it would take to wipe the scourge of lobbyists from the planet is electing politicians who don't accept bribes, but we clearly don't do that, so instead lobbying is a multibillion-dollar-a-year industry, and the world is falling apart, but it's okay because the reanimated corpse of Sheldon Adelson saved $400 million on his taxable liability.

HOW TO BECOME A LOBBYIST

Have older parents who are distant and too focused on their careers to pay you any attention or show you love. Pour all your energy into your academics and get an Ivy League education, or just lie and say you did. Contact a top lobbying firm and ask to speak to whoever's in charge; then threaten to publicly allege that they sexually assaulted you if they don't make you partner and give you a seven-figure salary and a corner office. The CEO will be so impressed with your innate ability to con and extort that they'll offer you an internship. Turn it down—they're bluffing—then send them some lewd pictures of their executives that you had Photoshopped. Then they'll play hard ball, and you can make a deal.

QUALIFICATIONS

- You're too slimy and unlikable for politics
- A punchable face

OCCUPATIONAL HAZARDS

- Having to live with yourself
- You'll hate what you do and find it soulless and corrupt but will make so much money that you can't bring yourself to leave because you're weak

Don't want to advance the interests of wealthy oligarchs?
Go to page 39.

Raise your risk
of dying in a
plane crash
by becoming a
fucking
**Flight
Attendant**

Back when America was still great—a period that lasted from August 11 to August 19, 1956—being a flight attendant was glamorous. They were respected and cosmopolitan and would jet-set around the globe like billionaires who occasionally had to serve refreshments and clean up uh-ohs in the lavatory. But then air travel became affordable, the plebs started flying, and now flight attendants are treated like air waitresses in a 1950s trophy wife costume by snippy, awful people who aren't trying to be rude, but if Parker doesn't get his apple juice right away, he's going to have a meltdown, and it will all be your fault. Flying is a terrifying experience that's technically safer than driving, except that with driving, if you get into a fatal crash, you usually die quickly, but with flying you spend minutes in abject terror, futilely trying to purchase Gogo Inflight Wi-Fi so you can text your family that you love them or stream your certain death live. You will fly all of the time, raising your statistical risk of death by being exploded into tiny pieces in a plane crash, and when you're not flying, you'll be in airports, airport hotels, or a rental apartment near your home because you grew apart from your significant other during all of your time away, and they asked that you move out so that they can get on with their life.

HOW TO BECOME A FLIGHT ATTENDANT

After 9/11, flight attendants' jobs changed from service to defense. Now all aspiring flight attendants must become experts in hand-to-hand combat, threat neutralization, and defusing bombs and small improvised explosive devices, in addition to being able to serve food and beverages and deal with passengers. Aspirants must spend two thousand hours on a flight simulator where something always goes wrong—engine failure, terrorist attacks, drunk racist white trash taking too many xannies and publicly spouting off nonsense—until they are finely honed killing machines.

QUALIFICATIONS

- Your rational fears don't include flying
- Basic knowledge of how seat belts work

OCCUPATIONAL HAZARDS

- Your butt will be goosed, you will be leered at and ogled, some man will try to force you into the bathroom for a quickie, and that's all before takeoff
- Flying

Don't want to die in a plane crash? Go to page 87.

Save hundreds of thousands of innocent lives annually by becoming a fucking **Trampoline Safety Attendant**

Trampolines are extremely fun, but they're also death traps that kill or maim approximately forty-five million people per year. That's why in 1981, a bipartisan commission set aside their petty differences to pass the binding Trampoline Related Accident and Mass-Casualty Prevention (TRAMP) Act, which appropriated government funding for an academy to research, study, and develop best practices around trampoline safety in order to protect America's most vital resource (other than oil and banking): its children. After a lengthy double-blind study in which seventy-nine of the one hundred members of the control group died from various orthopedic injuries, the researchers concluded that the best way to prevent catastrophe would be to have a trampoline safety attendant on site to demonstrate safe and proper trampoline usage, enforce the rules, and flirt with underage teens. A career was born, as was a new era in trampoline enjoyment, one in which only one-third of participants get severe life-altering injuries, a dramatic improvement over the pre–TRAMP Act levels. Trampoline safety attendants made it all possible, ensuring that nobody, or as few people as possible, die from broken necks by blowing their whistles at the first sign of danger, giving a stern look to unruly bouncers and/or horseplayers, and, in cases of extreme danger, yelling, "Hey!" and threatening to come over there but ultimately staying put.

HOW TO BECOME A TRAMPOLINE SAFETY ATTENDANT

To truly understand trampoline safety, you must first think like a trampoline; thus, prior to employment, all trampoline safety attendants are required to log one thousand hours of people jumping exuberantly on top of them so that they can learn the ins and outs of bouncing and see disaster before it strikes.

QUALIFICATIONS

- You are contractually obligated to comply anytime someone yells, "Do a backflip!"

- First aid and CPR certifications as well as a lack of squeamishness at the sight of blood or death

OCCUPATIONAL HAZARDS

- You may get burned by someone referring to the trampoline as your "mama-line"

- Paralysis

Can't do a gainer? Go to page 77.

Waste other people's money by becoming a fucking Interior Designer

Interior designers help the wealthy fool people into thinking they have good taste by dramatically transforming every room in their house into the expensive room that you weren't allowed to play in as a kid. They handle all aspects of a home's interior, from planning the best use of the space to finding new and innovative ways to blow through all of their clients' money. Interior design is basically a robbery where they also give your house a makeover. Designers get a percentage of every dollar they spend, so they'll work tirelessly to convince you that you definitely need a $56,000 horsehair mattress and dozens of $400 coffee table books. The most important thing you can do to become a successful interior designer is to already have close relationships with lots of rich people with bad taste; if you are able to rob ten rich people of even 1 percent of their net worth, that's a very nice living. Unfortunately, your customers are also your biggest competition, as every wealthy woman or gay man who's redecorated a room fancies themselves an interior designer, which is why it's important to always subtly emotionally manipulate your clients into believing that their taste is abhorrent and you're saving them from themselves.

HOW TO BECOME AN INTERIOR DESIGNER

Befriend a wealthy benefactor, and make them believe you're already a successful designer. When they invite you to their home, go on and on about your vision for it, even if they seem satisfied with their existing décor. Without their knowledge, order everything needed to make your dream a reality on credit, and when you know they'll be gone for an extended period, break in and redecorate. When they come home, they'll either have you arrested, which is a sign that you should consider a different career, or they'll be a combination of confused and not angry, in which case you're now an interior designer, so send them a bill for your design fee, plus everything you purchased with a 40 percent markup.

QUALIFICATIONS

- Good taste is considered a plus but not mandatory
- You are wealthy or know some wealthy

OCCUPATIONAL HAZARDS

- When the workers of the world unite and murder the rich, your business will likely decline
- You have to pretend to care about your clients' terrible ideas because they're paying you

Don't know any easily hoodwinked rich people? Go to page 17.